KU-303-685

Taste the seasons
with Lamona

HOWDENS
JOINERY CO.

MAKING SPACE MORE VALUABLE

howdens.com

LAMONA
Exclusive to Howdens Joinery Co.

lamona.co.uk

Taste the seasons with Lamona

Take your taste buds on a journey. Whether you are a keen cook or just starting to try your hand in the kitchen, these recipes will help you to create the right flavours from the seasons.

Enjoy the best dishes for spring, summer, autumn and winter with family and friends. All the recipes have been tested using Lamona appliances, so you can be confident they will turn out well.

The Lamona appliance range is all about choice and versatility and with these recipes, you will have many opportunities to discover all the great features of our products.

The Lamona Kitchen

Our Lamona kitchen incorporates the Linear style, creating a kitchen that is totally individual to you and your family's needs, whilst achieving an effortlessly stylish look. The island provides a real focal point without disturbing the simplicity of this design. With the Lamona pyrolytic oven and Lamona gas on glass hob you are able to cook the perfect dish for every season.

For a full range of our appliances available visit www.howdens.com/advice-inspiration/lamona-cookbook

Creating the perfect kitchen for cooking

When cooking and baking at home, you need to know that you can rely on your appliances. We offer plenty of choice from gas and electric hobs, microwaves, extractors, dishwashers, to fridges and freezers. Everything you need for your ideal kitchen.

With our exclusive Lamona appliances, you have all the reassurance you need. All our appliances are manufactured to the highest standards and come with a 2 year guarantee as standard. You can be sure that they are both durable and reliable as well as great value for money. Not surprisingly, Lamona is the biggest selling integrated appliance brand in the UK.

CHOOSING THE RIGHT OVEN

Our complete range of innovative integrated Lamona appliances means you will never need to compromise on functionality in your kitchen. Turning raw ingredients into delicious meals couldn't be easier with Lamona single and double ovens, microwaves and warming drawers. We are confident we have the right oven to suit both your style and culinary requirements.

EXTRACTORS

Whether you are looking for an additional focal point or want to hide it away we have a variety of extractors in various designs, features and functions to choose from. Positioned on a wall or centre of attention on an island, our Lamona range has an extractor to suit you.

HOBS

Choose a hob that suits your style and lifestyle. From the latest induction technology to traditional gas cooking features, we make finding the right hob for your kitchen easy. Choose between 2, 4 or 6 zone cooking areas and from gas, induction, ceramic and electric plates.

REFRIGERATION

Among our range of integrated fridge freezers, larder fridges and drink coolers you will find a large number of A++ rated appliances that can help you save money on household bills as well as being kind to the environment. Models have both frost free and fast freeze features available, which are designed to provide optimum storage conditions to keep your seasonal favourites fresh.

DISHWASHERS

Plan some extra help into your kitchen design with an integrated dishwasher. With a range of full sized and slimline energy efficient options to choose from, there is no reason why you can't have a little help with the washing up.

Our integrated dishwashers include advanced technology and their range of programmes provide outstanding wash and dry results every time.

Contents

Spring

Summer

Autumn

Winter

flavour
AT ITS BEST

Artichoke, Beetroot, Cabbage, Carrots, Chicory, Cucumber, Leeks, Parsnip, Purple Sprouting Broccoli, Radishes, Rhubarb, Sorrel, Spring Greens, Spring Onions, Watercress.

Put a spring in your step with seasonal greens

When spring is in full swing, it's time to liven up those meal choices. Use seasonal produce like fresh fruit, herbs, greens and other vegetables which are at their best at this time of year.

We have recipes that will awaken all your senses with vibrant colours and refreshing mouth-watering tastes. Our favourites are the Seafood Glass Noodle Salad, followed with the exotic Mango Pudding with Lime Syrup, delicious!

Seafood Glass Noodle Salad

Serves 4 **20 mins preparation,
10 mins cooking using the hob**

Ingredients

1 large celery stick, thinly sliced
⅓ cucumber, seeds removed,
thinly sliced
1½ teaspoons salt
1 small red onion, thinly sliced
120g green beans
300g mixed seafood, such as baby
octopus, squid and tiger prawns
100g glass noodles or rice
noodles, cooked to the pack
instructions, and cooled
160g baby plum tomatoes, halved
1 large lime leaf, finely chopped

For the dressing

2 garlic cloves, finely chopped
1-2 red chillies, seeds removed,
finely chopped
40ml lime juice
40ml fish sauce
2 tablespoons white sugar
1 teaspoon soy sauce
1 teaspoon sesame oil
1 small handful of coriander,
mint and Thai basil, torn
2 tablespoons chopped
plain peanuts

As the name suggests, glass noodles are translucent. They have a clean, refreshing flavour, so they're worth looking for – if you can't find them in your supermarket, you can use rice noodles instead.

1. Cook the noodles, following the instructions on the pack. When cooked, drain and keep to one side.

2. Put the celery and cucumber in a small bowl, and add ½ a teaspoon of salt. Mix lightly with your hands, and leave for 10 minutes.

3. Soak the red onion in a bowl of water for the same length of time, to release some of the bitterness.

4. Bring a small pan of water to the boil. Add ½ a teaspoon of salt and cook the green beans on a medium heat for 5 minutes. Drain, and gently cool down in cold water.

5. Bring another pan of water to the boil. Add ½ a teaspoon of salt and cook seafood for 2-3 minutes, until it's just cooked through. Drain though a sieve, and cool down in cold water.

6. In a large bowl, combine the noodles, tomatoes and chopped lime leaf, and keep to one side.

7. By now, the cucumber, celery and red onion should be ready. Squeeze out any excess water with your hands and add them to the large bowl.

8. Drain the cooled seafood and beans, pat dry with kitchen paper, and add them to the bowl too.

9. To make the dressing, combine the garlic, red chilli, lime juice, fish sauce, sugar, soy sauce and sesame oil in a small bowl. Mix thoroughly until the sugar has dissolved.

10. Pour the dressing over the salad and mix lightly with your hand. Arrange on a large plate to share, or on individual plates. Pour any remaining dressing from the bottom of the bowl over the top, and sprinkle with coriander, mint, Thai basil and chopped peanuts.

Curly Endive Salad

Serves 4 **15 mins preparation,
10 mins cooking using the hob**

Ingredients

1 small shallot
100g unsmoked bacon rashers
80g baguette
2 tablespoons red wine vinegar
Sea salt and milled black pepper
4 tablespoons groundnut or
grapeseed oil
2 tablespoons Dijon mustard
30g butter, melted
4 large eggs
200g curly endive or mixed
lettuce with curly endive

The secret of making a well-formed poached egg is ensuring it's very fresh – as an egg ages, the white tends to leave fine strands in the water. If you're not sure how fresh your eggs are, this foolproof recipe uses cling film to keep everything in shape. The rest of the salad is delicious too!

1. Bring a saucepan of water to a simmer.

2. Finely chop the shallot, and cut the bacon into 4cm chunks. Cut the baguette into 2cm cubes.

3. Make a vinaigrette by mixing the shallot, red wine vinegar, salt and pepper in a bowl. Slowly whisk in the oil, starting with half a teaspoon at a time. When all the oil is incorporated, whisk in the mustard. The vinaigrette should be thick but fluid. Keep to one side.

4. Cook the bacon in a frying pan over a medium heat for 2 minutes. Add the baguette cubes and cook for another 3 minutes, stirring occasionally, until you have crisp, golden croutons. Remove from the heat and keep covered.

5. Line a small bowl or a teacup with a 35cm square of cling film, and brush lightly with melted butter. Crack an egg in the centre. Gather the sides of the cling film, letting out all the air, and twist tightly. Repeat with the other eggs. Drop the cling-filmed eggs in the simmering water and cook for 6 minutes. Remove and keep to one side.

6. Mix the leaves and vinaigrette. Divide the salad between 4 plates and arrange the bacon and croutons on top. Carefully unwrap the eggs and place one on top of each salad.

Akuri

Serves 4   10 mins preparation, 10 mins cooking using the hob

Ingredients

2 tablespoons butter
1 red onion, finely diced
2 large garlic cloves, finely chopped
1 teaspoon ginger, grated
1 fresh red chilli, deseeded and finely sliced
2 teaspoons cumin seeds
1 large tomato, deseeded and finely chopped
1 handful fresh coriander leaves, finely chopped
6 large eggs, lightly beaten
100ml single cream or crème fraîche
Sea salt

To serve

Warm buttered toast

This quick spiced egg dish is perfect for a relaxed Sunday brunch. For a richer, creamier version, use four ducks eggs instead of the six large eggs.

1. Melt the butter in a large non-stick frying pan over a medium heat, and fry the onion for about 5 minutes, or until soft but not coloured.

2. Add the garlic, ginger, chilli and cumin seeds, and fry for a further minute.

3. Add half the tomato and half the coriander. Stir and cook gently for another minute.

4. Whisk the eggs with the single cream or crème fraîche, and season well with salt.

5. Take the pan off the heat, and pour in the egg mixture. Return the pan to a medium-low heat, and stir with a wooden spoon until the mixture is slightly set – it should have a creamy texture and will take about 6-8 minutes.

6. Quickly stir in the remaining tomato and coriander.

7. Serve immediately over slices of freshly buttered toast.

Roasted Pepper, Taleggio and Sun-Blushed Tomato Frittata

Serves 6 **10 mins preparation,
20 mins cooking using the hob and oven**

Ingredients

400g new potatoes
6 large free range eggs,
lightly beaten
200g jar roasted red peppers,
drained and sliced into strips
150g Taleggio cheese, rind
removed and cubed
1 large handful fresh basil
100g sun-blushed
tomatoes, halved
2 tablespoons extra virgin
olive oil

To serve

50g rocket leaves
Juice of ½ lemon
Sea salt

Taleggio is a creamy, flavourful cheese that melts beautifully into this frittata – an Italian-style omelette, best enjoyed at room temperature.

1. Place the potatoes in a medium saucepan and cover with water. Bring to the boil and cook for 7 minutes until tender. Drain and let them cool.

2. When the potatoes are cool enough to handle, use a sharp knife to cut into slices, about the thickness of a pound coin.

3. Add the beaten eggs to the potatoes, along with the strips of pepper, cubes of cheese, most of the basil, and the tomatoes. Gently fold everything together.

4. Pre-heat the grill to medium.

5. Heat half the extra virgin olive oil over a low heat in a 23cm non-stick frying pan, and gently tip in the egg mixture. Cook very gently for 10-12 minutes, until nearly set.

6. Place the frying pan under the grill to finish cooking for a further 3-4 minutes, until the frittata is set and golden.

7. Place the rocket leaves and remaining basil in a bowl, and toss with the lemon juice, remaining extra virgin olive oil and a pinch of salt.

8. Cut the frittata into wedges, and serve with the rocket and basil salad.

Roasted Pepper, Taleggio and Sun-Blushed Tomato Frittata | 21

Rare Beef Pho

Serves 4 · 5 mins preparation, 25 mins cooking using the hob and oven

Ingredients

200g dried rice noodles, about 5mm width
1 star anise
2 cardamom pods, crushed
½ cinnamon stick
4 shallots, skins on, quartered
4 garlic cloves, crushed
2 teaspoons vegetable oil
4 large slices of ginger
2 teaspoons black peppercorns
2 spring onions, roughly chopped
1.2 litres organic beef stock
(either freshly made or diluted stock cubes)
½ teaspoon white sugar
1 lime leaf
1 teaspoon fish sauce
Salt and white pepper to season
200g beef fillet, finely sliced
½ onion, finely sliced and soaked in water
100g beansprouts
1 bird's eye chilli, finely sliced
4 lime wedges
2 spring onions, finely sliced
1 handful chopped coriander, mint, shiso or Thai basil

Pho is a popular street food in Vietnam. It is made from rice noodles in a light, fragrant broth with chicken, beef or pork stock and topped with tender rare beef fillet slices.

1. Pre-heat the oven to 240°C/fan 220°C/gas mark 9.

2. Place the rice noodles in a large bowl and pour enough warm water over to cover them. Leave for 20-25 minutes, until the noodles are fairly soft.

3. Place the star anise, cardamom pods and cinnamon stick on a small metal baking tray, and dry roast them in the oven for 3 minutes.

4. Put the shallots and garlic on a separate baking tray, and smear with oil. Cook in the oven for 10 minutes.

5. Meanwhile, transfer the roasted spices to a large pan, and add the ginger, black peppercorns, roughly cut spring onions and beef stock. Bring to the boil on the highest heat.

6. When the shallots and garlic are soft, add them to the pan. Turn down the heat and simmer gently for 5-10 minutes.

7. Pour the broth through a sieve to remove the spices. Discard the spices and pour the liquid back in the pan. Simmer again on a low heat and add the sugar, fish sauce and lime leaf. Taste, and, if necessary, adjust the flavour by adding a little more fish sauce or a pinch of salt. Season with white pepper.

8. Drain the noodles and cook them in the broth for 1-2 minutes, until they're soft enough to eat. Divide them between the 4 warmed bowls.

9. Put the fillet slices on top of the noodles, and pour the piping hot broth over. Arrange the onion slices, beansprouts, chilli slices, lime wedges and spring onions on each bowl, and scatter with plenty of green herbs. Eat while it's hot.

Salmon with Goat's Cheese and Watercress Sauce

Serves 4   10 mins preparation, 15 mins cooking using the hob and oven

Ingredients

4 x 170g salmon fillets with the skins on
1 tablespoon olive oil
Sea salt and milled black pepper to season
125g soft goat's cheese
125g Greek yogurt
60ml water
60g watercress, finely chopped

To serve

Green beans

Watercress and goat's cheese sauce is a classic accompaniment for salmon. Together with the crispy salmon skin and slightly "pink" salmon centre, makes this dish simply delicious.

1. Pre-heat the oven to 200°C/fan 180°C/gas mark 6. Line a baking tray with kitchen foil.

2. Heat a large, non-stick frying pan. Brush the salmon fillets with a little oil and season well. Place them in the pan and cook, skin side down, over a medium heat for 2 minutes. Flip them over and cook for 2 more minutes.

3. Transfer the fillets to the baking tray, skin side down, and bake for 8 minutes if you like it slightly pink at the heart, or 10 minutes if you like it more cooked.

4. Meanwhile, mash together the goat's cheese, yogurt and water until smooth. Transfer to a small saucepan and warm gently. Add the watercress, and cook over a low heat for a couple of minutes, until it starts to wilt. Don't let it boil, or the mixture will curdle. Season to taste and leave to infuse.

5. For a smoother texture and a lovely green colour, give it a whiz in the food processor or with an electric hand blender.

6. Place the salmon fillets on plates, drizzle the sauce on top and serve with green beans.

Ligurian Trofie Pasta

Serves 4   **5 mins preparation,
15-20 mins cooking using the hob**

Ingredients
350g Trofie pasta or any
short pasta
250g small new potatoes, halved
100g fine green beans
4 tablespoons basil pesto sauce
(see below)
4 tablespoons Parmesan cheese,
finely grated

Trofie are short, thin, knotted strips of pasta, so pesto sauce is a perfect partner. Of course, you can buy decent ready-made pesto but making your own is pretty easy, and gives the finished dish extra depth of flavour.

1. Bring a large pan of water to the boil. Add the pasta and cook for 5 minutes, until it starts to soften.

2. Add the new potatoes and cook for 5 minutes more, then add the green beans and cook for a final 3-4 minutes until tender.

3. Drain the pasta, potatoes and beans, saving a ladleful of the cooking water, and return to the pan.

4. Add the pesto sauce and a little of the cooking water. Stir well, then sprinkle with the Parmesan and serve immediately.

Basil Pesto Sauce

Serves 4   **10 mins preparation**

Ingredients
1 small garlic clove
1 pinch sea salt
25g pine nuts, very lightly toasted
50g fresh basil
25g Parmesan cheese, finely grated
Juice of ½ lemon
75ml extra virgin olive oil

1. Place the garlic in a pestle and mortar with the sea salt, and pound until you've crushed the garlic to a paste. Add the pine nuts and basil, and continue to pound until you have a coarse paste (if you prefer, you can do this stage in a food processor).

2. Transfer the paste to a bowl, and stir in the Parmesan, lemon juice and extra virgin olive oil – along with enough water to make a thick sauce.

Fresh pesto can be made in advance and stored in the fridge in a sealed container with a thin layer of olive oil on the top for up to 5 days.

Mango Pudding with Lime Syrup

Serves 4-6   5 mins preparation, 25 mins cooking using the microwave and fridge

Ingredients

6 sheets gelatine
690ml water
3 tablespoons hot water
6 tablespoons white sugar
1 tablespoon lime juice
450ml sweetened Alphonso mango purée
6 tablespoons evaporated milk

For the syrup

4 tablespoons milk or water
3 tablespoons white sugar
6 tablespoons evaporated milk
2 tablespoons lime juice

To serve

Sprigs of mint
1 fresh mango, sliced

This sweet, creamy pudding is a popular way to eat mangoes in South East Asia. Serve with lime syrup poured over, to make this dish a taste sensation.

1. In a jug or bowl, add the gelatine sheets to 600ml water and soak for 5 minutes.

2. Squeeze the water out with your hands, and place the gelatine in a small microwavable bowl. Add 90ml of water and put cling film over the bowl. Microwave on full power for 10 seconds. Make sure the gelatine has dissolved – if not, give it 5 more seconds.

3. Combine 3 tablespoons of hot water with the sugar, making sure the sugar dissolves completely. Then add the lime juice and pour into the gelatine mix, stirring well.

4. Pour three quarters of the mango purée into a bowl, adding the remaining quarter to the sugar and gelatine mix, and pour back into the bowl of mango purée.

5. Add the evaporated milk and mix thoroughly. Divide the mixture between 4 jelly moulds.

6. Place the moulds in a deep container, large enough to take all four. Put crushed ice and cold water around the moulds, and place the container in the fridge. The gelatine should be set in about 20-25 minutes.

7. Meanwhile, to make the syrup, pour the milk or water into a small microwavable bowl, and put cling film over the top. Microwave on full power for 10 seconds, and then add the sugar. Stir to dissolve the sugar, and then add the evaporated milk. Leave to cool slightly and then add the lime juice, stirring frequently with a small whisk to avoid curdling.

8. To check whether the puddings are ready, touch the tops lightly – they shouldn't stick to your finger.

9. Dip the moulds in hot water for 2-3 seconds, and turn out the puddings onto plates. Pour the lime syrup over the top, and decorate each one with a sprig of mint and sliced fresh mango.

Coconut Macaroons

Makes 12 **5 mins preparation, 15 mins cooking using the oven**

Ingredients
2 egg whites
90g caster sugar
150g desiccated coconut

These little bites come from the French Antilles in the Caribbean. High-temperature baking makes them crispy outside and deliciously moist inside. A wonderful way to use leftover egg whites.

1. Pre-heat the oven to 220°C/fan 200°C/gas mark 7. Line a baking tray with baking parchment.

2. Place all the ingredients in a medium-size saucepan and mix well. Cook over a very low heat for 3 minutes, until the mixture becomes sticky but no more than slightly hot to the touch. Transfer to a bowl and leave to cool for 2 minutes.

3. When still warm but cool enough to handle, squeeze a tablespoon of the mixture in your palm to form a small ball with a slight point. Repeat to make 12 macaroons, placing them on the lined baking tray.

4. Bake for 10 minutes, until dark brown on the outside.

Pineapple Jam Tart

Serves 4 **10 mins preparation, 20 mins cooking using the hob and oven**

Ingredients

400g fresh pineapple
(skinned and cored weight)
10g butter
50g white sugar
1 star anise
½ cinnamon stick
1 roll of ready-made sweet or
Shortcrust pastry
1 egg, lightly beaten with
1 tablespoon water

Fresh pineapple jam, fragrant with hints of cinnamon and star anise, contrasts with the rich pastry, giving you a perfectly balanced sweet treat. It's great with a cup of tea.

1. Chop the pineapple roughly and put the pieces in a food processor or blender to make a purée. Put this through a fine sieve, using a spatula to separate the pulp from the juice.

2. Melt the butter in a frying pan and fry the pineapple pulp to make a thick paste, stirring frequently.

3. Pour the pineapple juice into a small pan and add the sugar, star anise and cinnamon stick. Heat on medium to low, until the volume reduces by about three quarters. When it's very condensed, remove the star anise and cinnamon and add the pan-fried pulp to make a thick jam.

4. Spread the jam on a metal baking tray to cool down.

5. Pre-heat the oven to 190°C/fan 170°C/gas mark 5. Roll out the pastry, and cut out 24 round discs, 5cm in diameter. Put 12 of them on a large baking tray lined with baking parchment and brush with egg wash.

6. Use a 3cm round cutter to cut the centres out of the remaining 12 discs. Place each of the circles you've made on the top of the first 12 pastry discs, and push the edges with a fork to make patterns like sun rays.

7. Fill a bowl with water. Use this to keep wetting your hands as you divide the pineapple filling into 12 balls. Place each ball in the centre of a pastry, and flatten it slightly. (If you have time, make thin strips from the leftover pastry and use these to create criss-cross patterns on top, and brush with egg wash).

8. Put the tarts in the oven and cook for 15-20 minutes, until they're lightly browned. Let them cool down slightly before serving.

Masala Chai

Serves 4   **5 mins preparation,
7 mins cooking using the hob**

Ingredients

500ml water
200ml milk
50g caster sugar
2 cinnamon sticks
6 cloves
6 green cardamom pods,
lightly crushed
2 slices ginger
1-2 tablespoons Assam
loose-leaf tea

This Indian tea is made by brewing black tea with a mixture of aromatic spices and herbs.

1. Pour the water and milk into a saucepan with the sugar, cinnamon sticks, cloves, cardamom pods and ginger. Bring to the boil, reduce the heat to low, and simmer for 5-6 minutes.

2. Put the tea leaves in a teapot and pour in the spiced mixture. Allow to infuse for 4-5 minutes, then using a strainer, pour into teacups.

Lemongrass and Ginger Tea

Serves 4   **5 mins preparation,
6-8 mins cooking using the hob**

Ingredients

4 stalks lemongrass,
plus extra to garnish
1 small knob of ginger,
thinly sliced
600ml water
1 green tea bag

To serve

Honey

This drink has a delicate floral aroma. It's the perfect afternoon pick-me-up and very soothing after dinner as an alternative to coffee.

1. Cut the lemongrass into 4cm lengths and crush with the flat side of a large knife. Place in a saucepan with the ginger and water.

2. Bring to the boil and add the green tea bag. Take the pan off the heat and allow the tea to infuse for 3-4 minutes.

3. Using a fine sieve or strainer, pour the tea into heatproof glasses or cups.

4. Garnish with stalks of lemongrass and serve with honey to sweeten.

Summer Lovin'

Long summer days leave us yearning for big, bright flavours that delight your senses and quench your thirst. Whether you are having a dinner party or a BBQ, we have a selection of flavoursome but simple dishes for you to impress your guests with, including Broad Bean, Mint and Lemon Salad, Crispy Fried Chicken and Strawberries with Mascarpone Cream all washed down with vibrantly fruity Mimosas.

flavour
AT ITS BEST

Apricots, Bell Peppers,
Cherries, Corn, Cucumber,
Garlic, Lemons, Limes, Melons,
Nectarines, Peaches, Plums,
Radishes, Strawberries,
Tomatoes.

Broad Bean, Mint and Lemon Salad

Serves 4 **15 mins preparation, 5 mins cooking using the oven and hob**

Ingredients

8 thin slices pancetta
350g freshly shelled or frozen broad beans
1 garlic clove
2 tablespoons extra virgin olive oil, plus extra for drizzling
Juice and grated zest of ½ lemon
Sea salt and milled black pepper
1 large handful fresh mint, chopped
4 slices sourdough bread

This fresh-tasting salad is best when broad beans are in season, if you can't get them fresh, frozen beans are a good substitute. Either way, the mint enhances the freshness of the beans, and the saltiness of the pancetta balances all the flavours beautifully.

1. Pre-heat the grill to high.

2. Lay the pancetta on a rack inside the grill tray. Grill for 4-5 minutes, until lightly golden and crisp. Put to one side to cool.

3. Bring a large pan of salted water to the boil. Add the beans and cook for 2-3 minutes if they're fresh, or 4 minutes if they're frozen – they should be just tender.

4. Drain the beans well, refresh them in cold water, and drain again.

5. To make the dressing, crush half the garlic clove. Place it in a small bowl, and whisk together with the extra virgin olive oil, lemon juice and zest, a pinch of salt and plenty of pepper.

6. To serve, drizzle the dressing over the beans, add the mint, and gently toss together. Toast the sourdough slices, then rub the remaining garlic over them and drizzle with a little oil. Place one slice of bread on each of 4 serving plates and pile the beans on top. Add 2 pancetta slices to each one, and serve immediately.

Fresh Anchovy Fritto Misto

Serves 4   10 mins preparation, 5 mins cooking using the oven and hob

Ingredients

400g fresh anchovies
1 lemon
3 tablespoons flat-leaf parsley, very finely chopped
50g plain flour
50g cornflour
50g fine polenta
1 pinch cayenne pepper
Sea salt and milled black pepper
1 litre olive oil

Fresh anchovies have a deliciously mild, fresh flavour compared to the salted, canned variety. They're amazing served like this, quickly fried and piping hot for a real taste of the Mediterranean. Traditionally, small fresh anchovies can be eaten whole, but ask your fishmonger to gut and debone any larger ones.

1. Pre-heat the oven to 150ºC/fan 130ºC/gas mark 2.

2. Line a large baking tray with plenty of kitchen paper.

3. Place the anchovies in a shallow dish. Squeeze over the juice of half a lemon, and sprinkle with 2 tablespoons of the chopped parsley.

4. In another shallow dish, mix together the flour, cornflour, polenta and cayenne pepper. Season well with a pinch of salt and plenty of pepper.

5. In an electric deep fryer or large pan, heat the olive oil to 190ºC. (To test the temperature, put a cube of bread in the pan. At 190ºC, it will brown in 30 seconds).

6. Coat the anchovies in the flour mixture, and shake off any excess. In small batches, place in the hot oil and fry for 1 minute, until crisp and lightly golden.

7. Use a slotted spoon to lift the anchovies onto the paper-lined baking tray. Keep warm in the oven while you prepare and cook the rest.

8. Serve scattered with the remaining parsley and wedges of lemon.

Crispy Fried Chicken

Serves 4 **5 mins preparation,
25 mins cooking using the hob**

Ingredients

800g chicken wings
(or 700g chicken thighs)
2 tablespoons white or red wine
½ teaspoon grated ginger
¼ teaspoon grated garlic
¼ teaspoon sea salt
60g cornflour
½ tablespoon baking powder
1 litre vegetable or groundnut oil

For the sauce

1½ tablespoons soy sauce
4 tablespoons mirin (sweet
rice wine) or sake (rice wine)
2½ tablespoons rice wine vinegar
1½ tablespoons chilli paste
3 tablespoons honey
3 teaspoons sesame oil
2 tablespoons light brown sugar
1 teaspoon grated ginger

To serve (optional)

A few handfuls of peanuts,
or toasted sesame seeds
Salad leaves

This is a simple, finger-licking dish that is perfect for entertaining family or friends. It's crispy fried chicken with a sticky, sweet and spicy coating.

1. Put all the chicken pieces in a large bowl and add the wine, ginger and garlic. Mix well with your hands and leave for at least 5 minutes.

2. Combine the salt, cornflour and baking powder in a bowl, mix well with a spoon.

3. Add the flour mix to the chicken, and use your hands to make sure the chicken is well coated. Arrange the pieces on a plate or baking tray.

4. Pour the oil into a deep fryer or wok and heat to 180°C.

5. While the oil is heating, make the sauce by mixing all the ingredients in a small bowl. (You can make the sauce in advance, and keep it in the fridge for up to a week).

6. When the oil is hot, carefully lower in the chicken pieces and fry until they turn golden. If you want to do this in batches, drain each batch on kitchen paper and keep it warm while you do the rest.

7. Once all the chicken is cooked, put the sauce into a large, clean wok or frying pan over a medium heat. When it starts to bubble, add the crispy fried chicken, and coat it evenly with the sticky sweet sauce.

8. Top with peanuts or toasted sesame seeds, and serve with salad leaves.

44 | Mango Chicken

Mango Chicken

Serves 4 **15 mins preparation,
15 mins cooking using the hob**

Ingredients

For the marinade

¼ teaspoon ground coriander
1 teaspoon grated ginger
1 teaspoon grated garlic
1½ tablespoons cornflour
4 teaspoons soy sauce
1 teaspoon white sugar

For the sauce

3 tablespoons tomato ketchup
60ml chicken or vegetable stock
2 teaspoons white sugar
2 teaspoons soy sauce

For the rest of the recipe

400g boneless chicken thighs,
cut into 1-inch chunks
¼ teaspoon cumin seeds,
lightly toasted and crushed
2 tablespoons lime juice
1 tablespoon white sugar
300g fresh mango
(without the stone), peeled
and cut into chunks
1 large carrot,
peeled and sliced diagonally
1 large onion, cut into 1-inch cubes
1 red pepper, cut into 1-inch squares
2 tablespoons vegetable oil
1 red chilli, deseeded and
sliced (optional)
1 small handful cashew nuts
A few spring onions to garnish

This American influenced Malaysian dish is similar to Chinese sweet and sour, but uses mango chunks instead of pineapple. It's really easy to make your own sweet and sour sauce from scratch – and it's nice to try this different way of cooking chicken.

1. In a large bowl, mix all the marinade ingredients apart from the chicken.

2. Make sure there are no lumps of cornflour, and then add the chicken. Cover with cling film and marinade for 10 minutes.

3. In a small bowl, mix all the ingredients for the additional sauce.

4. Put the cumin, lime juice and sugar in a bowl and add the mango chunks. Mix thoroughly.

5. Bring a large pan of hot water to the boil, add the carrot and cook for 1 minute, then add the onion and red pepper. Cook for another minute and drain in a colander.

6. Place a wok over a high heat and add the oil. Fry the cashew nuts for a few minutes until golden, then take them out of the oil and drain on kitchen paper.

7. If you're using the red chilli, fry it in the same oil for 30 seconds, then add the chicken. Cook for 3-4 minutes over a high heat, until it turns brown. Add the carrot, onion and red pepper and cook for another 3 minutes, or until the onion has become lightly brown.

8. Add the sauce and mango. Fry for a few more minutes, until the sauce thickens slightly.

9. Top with the cashew nuts and spring onions and serve with plain boiled rice.

Dover Sole with Capers and Brown Shrimps

Serves 2   **10 mins preparation,
10 mins cooking using the oven and hob**

Ingredients

3 tablespoons capers in vinegar
2 tablespoons plain flour
¼ teaspoon milled black pepper
2 x 300g Dover sole (ask the
fishmonger to remove the brown
skin and scale the white)
80g lightly salted butter, melted
1 banana shallot, finely chopped
80g cooked brown shrimps
or tiny prawns, peeled

To serve

1 lemon, halved
Steamed potatoes

Dover sole is a lovely treat and with this easy, under-the-grill method, you don't have to flip the fish over. The caper and brown shrimp butter is quick to prepare too. If you can't get hold of brown shrimps, you can use small prawns instead.

1. Pre-heat the grill to maximum. Line the oven tray with kitchen foil and place under the grill.

2. Rinse and drain the capers.

3. Mix the flour and black pepper, and spread on a large plate, the size of the fish.

4. Dry the sole with kitchen paper, and dip in the flour until lightly coated on both sides.

5. Take the hot tray from the grill. Brush it carefully with melted butter and lay the fish, white skin side down, on the tray. Drizzle a couple of tablespoons of butter over the top of each sole, slide the tray in the lowest rack and grill for 9 to 10 minutes. You know they're cooked when the flesh comes away easily from the bone.

6. While the fish is cooking, fry the chopped shallot in 2 tablespoons of butter for 2 minutes. Add the capers and fry for 1 more minute, until they puff up.

7. Add the shrimps or prawns, and cook for 30-60 seconds, just to reheat them.

8. Remove the sole from the oven and transfer to 2 plates. Drizzle with the sauce, and serve with lemon halves and steamed potatoes.

Spaghetti with Broad Beans, Tomatoes and Creamy Goat's Cheese

Serves 4   **10 mins preparation,
15 mins cooking using the hob**

Ingredients

200g fresh broad beans (shelled weight)
2 tablespoons extra virgin olive oil
300g cherry tomatoes, quartered
2 garlic cloves, finely chopped
400g spaghetti
200g fresh baby spinach leaves
100g fresh mild goat's cheese, chopped

This light, fresh-flavoured pasta dish takes hardly any cooking, so it's great for a quick (but quite special) lunch.

1. Bring a medium pan of water to the boil, and blanch the broad beans for a minute. Drain well and run under cold water. Remove the outer skins to reveal the bright green flesh.

2. Heat the extra virgin olive oil in a saucepan, and add the cherry tomatoes and garlic. Cook until the tomatoes are really soft and the garlic is lightly golden. Take the pan off the heat.

3. Bring a large pan of water to the boil, and cook the spaghetti according to the packet instructions. Drain and return it to the pan.

4. While the pasta is still hot, quickly add the tomatoes and garlic, spinach, broad beans and goat's cheese. Toss together gently, and serve immediately with a drizzle of extra virgin olive oil.

Spaghetti with Broad Beans, Tomatoes and Creamy Goat's Cheese | 49

Mussels in White Wine Sauce

Serves 4   **15 mins preparation,
10 mins cooking using the hob**

Ingredients

2.5kg mussels
60g butter
100g shallots, finely chopped
1 stick celery, finely chopped
3 garlic cloves, finely chopped
50g parsley, chopped
300ml white wine
(preferably Muscadet)
Milled black pepper

To serve

Crusty bread or french fries

You can prepare mussels in lots of ways, but this simple approach, with shallots, celery, parsley and white wine is refreshing for the summer.

1. Warm a serving dish and 4 plates in your oven, on its lowest setting.

2. Wash the mussels under cold water, discarding any opened or damaged ones. Remove the 'beards', the seaweed-like strands attached to the side, by pulling them towards the pointed end of the shell.

3. Melt half the butter in the pot. Add the shallots and celery, and cook over a medium heat for 3 minutes, until soft. Add the garlic and half the parsley, and cook for 30 seconds.

4. Add the wine and bring to a boil. Increase the heat to maximum and add the mussels. Cover the pot and cook for 4-5 minutes, stirring occasionally, until all the mussels have opened. Turn off the heat and leave to sit for a couple of minutes.

5. Transfer the mussels to the warm serving dish by spooning them in rather than pouring them out (so the cooking liquid stays in the pot). Keep them warm in the oven.

6. Pass the cooking liquid through a fine sieve to remove any grit or dirt, then pour it into a saucepan and bring to a simmer.

7. Whisk in the rest of the butter and parsley, and add lots of black pepper.

8. Pour the sauce over the mussels and serve at once with crusty bread or french fries.

Lemon Curd and Cream Roly-Poly

Serves 4-6   15 mins preparation, 15 mins baking using the oven

Ingredients

4 egg whites
1 pinch fine sea salt
90g caster sugar
6 egg yolks
25g plain flour
25g cornflour
300ml whipping cream
2 tablespoons icing sugar
Grated zest and juice of 1 lemon
1 teaspoon honey
350g good quality lemon curd

To serve

Icing sugar

In this recipe we use lemon curd, but you could use jam, chocolate hazelnut spread, chestnut cream or fruit compote.

1. Pre-heat the oven to 220°C/fan 200°/gas mark 7. Line a baking tray with a sheet of baking parchment.

2. Beat the egg whites with a pinch of salt until they form soft peaks. With the beaters still running, slowly add 40g of the sugar. When the whites are glossy and stiff, beat for 20 seconds more and then put to one side.

3. Add the remaining 50g of sugar to the egg yolks and beat for exactly 2 minutes, until foamy and light in colour.

4. Carefully fold the yolk mixture into the beaten whites in 2 batches, swirling and lifting gently to avoid breaking the air bubbles.

5. Add the flour and cornflour in the same way.

6. Pour the batter onto the lined baking tray and spread delicately into a 25 x 35cm rectangle. Bake for 8 minutes until puffed and golden.

7. Remove the sponge from the oven, lift it by the baking parchment and place on a rack. Cover with a clean tea towel to cool.

8. Meanwhile, whip the cream, icing sugar and grated zest of half the lemon – until not quite, but almost, stiff.

9. Squeeze the lemon and mix the juice with the honey.

10. Flip the cake over onto a second sheet of baking parchment. Peel the paper off the upturned base by rolling it close to the cake surface rather than lifting it; this avoids damaging the sponge.

11. Drizzle the sponge with the lemon juice and honey mixture. Spread a layer of lemon curd over the surface, followed by a layer of the whipped cream mixture, leaving a 2cm gap around the edges.

12. Roll the sponge tightly from the short end, lifting the paper to help the rolling. Transfer it to a serving plate and leave to cool in the fridge. Serve sliced with a dusting of icing sugar.

Strawberries with Balsamic Syrup and Mascarpone Cream

Serves 4 **10 mins preparation,
5 mins cooking using the hob**

Ingredients

300g strawberries
50g caster sugar
4 tablespoons balsamic vinegar
150ml whipping cream
150g mascarpone
2 tablespoons icing sugar
1 small handful basil leaves

Balsamic vinegar really enhances the flavour of strawberries, especially when made into a sweet syrup. And with this creamy mascarpone topping, you have the perfect summer dessert.

1. Hull the strawberries (remove the green top and core). Slice and place in a large bowl.

2. Place the sugar and balsamic vinegar in a small saucepan over a medium heat, and bring to a gentle simmer. Cook for 5 minutes, until the volume reduces by half.

3. Whip the cream, mascarpone and icing sugar together, until you have a thick, creamy, spoonable mixture.

4. Spoon the strawberries into serving bowls. Drizzle over the balsamic syrup, and top with a spoonful of mascarpone cream and a few basil leaves.

Mimosa

Serves 1   **5 mins preparation**

Ingredients

100ml freshly
squeezed orange juice
1½ teaspoons Cointreau
60ml Champagne, chilled
Orange slices to garnish

The French lay claim to this cocktail, created in 1925 at the Ritz in Paris. But really it's a take on the Buck's Fizz, invented four years earlier in London at the Buck's Club.

1. Pour the orange juice and Cointreau into a Champagne flute.

2. Hold the glass at an angle and slowly pour in the Champagne. The mixture will froth, so fill the glass half way and wait for a few seconds before topping up with more Champagne.

3. Decorate with a slice of orange and serve.

Cheese Twists

Serves 4
(12 Twists)

10 mins preparation,
10 mins baking using the oven

Ingredients

1 egg
1 pinch sea salt
60g Gruyère cheese
320g pack ready rolled
all butter puff pastry
1½ tablespoons Dijon mustard
1 nutmeg
Milled black pepper

Cheese twists are always a favourite to nibble with drinks and much nicer when they're freshly baked. This recipe is pepped up with a touch of mustard and grated nutmeg.

1. Pre-heat the oven to 220°C/fan 200°C/gas mark 7. Line a baking tray with baking parchment.

2. Whisk the egg lightly with a good pinch of salt. Finely grate the cheese.

3. Unroll the puff pastry on the work surface. Cut in half, keeping one half in the fridge for another recipe. Brush the half you're using with egg, and spread with mustard.

4. Sprinkle the cheese evenly over the top, pressing it down, so it sticks to the surface. Grate nutmeg generously over the cheese, and season with freshly milled black pepper.

5. Cut the pastry into twelve 1.5cm strips, along the shorter side.

6. Lift a strip, twist it, then transfer it to the lined baking tray. Press both ends lightly into the parchment to help the twist hold its shape.

7. Repeat, until you have 12 strips arranged on the baking tray. Brush any bare pastry (the bits without cheese) with egg and bake for 9-10 minutes, until well puffed and golden. Serve warm or cold.

Tip: You can also bake these untwisted, as flat cheese straws.

flavour
AT ITS BEST

Apples, Blackberries, Brussel
Sprouts, Butternut Squash,
Cabbages, Carrots, Cauliflowers,
Celery, Kale, Leeks, Onions,
Parsnip, Pears, Potatoes,
Pumpkins, Spinach, Turnips.

Autumn recipes we've fallen for...

Autumn evenings are extra special when you can come home to delicious aromas baking in the kitchen. You yearn for depth, complexity and flavours built from layers of ingredients and slow cooking. Tuck into our seasonal selection of comforting recipes such as Pork Saltimbocca, Duck Legs in Orange Sauce and Porcini Risotto. Our Apple Tart and Rice Pudding with Warm Cherry Sauce finish the night off perfectly.

Smoked Salmon with Beetroot, Red Onion and Capers on Rye

Serves 4   15 mins preparation

Ingredients

4 tablespoons crème fraîche
2 tablespoons fresh dill, finely chopped
Juice and zest of 1 small lemon
Sea salt and milled black pepper
4 slices rye bread
4 slices smoked salmon
2 cooked beetroot, finely diced
½ red onion, peeled and finely sliced
4 small pickled gherkins, finely sliced lengthways
1 teaspoon capers, drained
1 tablespoon fresh chives, finely chopped

Use smoked salmon mixed with a variety of flavoursome ingredients to create the perfect open sandwich. Alternatively, try it for brunch with a poached egg.

1. In a small bowl, mix together the crème fraîche, dill and lemon zest. Season with salt and pepper and keep to one side.

2. Place each slice of rye bread on a plate and spread with the crème fraîche mixture.

3. Top each one with a slice of smoked salmon and sprinkle with beetroot, red onion, gherkins and capers.

4. Drizzle with lemon juice and scatter with chives. Season with salt and pepper, and serve immediately.

Baked Eggs with Tarragon

Serves 2 — **5 mins preparation, 17 mins cooking using the oven**

Ingredients

15g butter, melted
4 medium eggs
2 tablespoons tarragon, chopped
2 tablespoons crème fraîche
Sea salt and milled black pepper
2 slices rye sourdough bread,
toasted, buttered and cut into strips

In this recipe the eggs are baked in a ramekin, traditionally in a 'bain-marie' (water bath). But this is a much easier way to get a nice set, white and runny yolk – perfect for a romantic breakfast treat.

1. Pre-heat the oven to 200°C/fan 180°C/gas mark 6.

2. Brush the inside of each ramekin with melted butter.

3. Crack 2 eggs over each ramekin, letting the white fall and keeping the yolks in the shell, being careful not to break them. Place the half shells with the yolks back in the egg box for later.

4. Place the ramekins on a small baking tray and bake for 10 minutes. Remove from the oven, and sprinkle each one with a tablespoon of tarragon. Top each ramekin with 2 of the reserved egg yolks and a tablespoon of crème fraîche. Season well.

5. Return the ramekins to the oven and bake for a further 7 minutes. Serve them straight out of the oven with the buttered toast. Be careful, the ramekins will be hot!

Tip: You can add anything you fancy with the egg yolks and crème fraîche – such as smoked salmon, cooked spinach, cooked mushrooms or grated cheese.

Onion, Bacon and Cream Tart

Serves 4   10 mins preparation, 20 mins baking using the oven and hob

Ingredients

3 medium egg yolks
2 pinches sea salt
320g pack ready rolled
all butter puff pastry
1 red onion
100g smoked streaky bacon
150g fromage frais
150g crème fraîche
¼ teaspoon nutmeg,
freshly grated
Milled black pepper

To serve

Green salad

This delicious alternative to the classic pizza, was made traditionally from scraps of bread to test the heat of the wood-fired oven while waiting for the main loaf to prove. This version is equally delicious, using a puff pastry base and crème fraîche, which gives a lovely smooth texture when it cooks.

1. Pre-heat the oven to 200°C/fan 180°C/gas mark 6. Line the oven tray with baking parchment.

2. Mix the three egg yolks with a large pinch of salt.

3. Unroll the pastry, prick with a fork and place on the prepared oven tray. Using the tip of a knife, mark a line around the pastry, 1 centimetre inside the edge. Lightly brush with some of the salted egg yolk mixture, place in the oven on the lowest shelf and bake for 10 minutes.

4. Meanwhile, finely slice the onion, and fry the bacon in a large frying pan over a high heat for 2 minutes. Mix the fromage frais, crème fraîche, egg yolks and nutmeg with a large pinch of salt and around 10 turns of the peppermill, to suit your taste.

5. Remove the puff pastry from the oven and turn up the temperature to 220°C/fan 200°C/gas mark 7.

6. Press the centre of the pastry, inside the knife markings, with the back of a spoon to create a contained space for the topping. Spread the fromage frais mixture over the recessed surface. Arrange the sliced onion on top, then the cooked bacon.

7. Bake for 10 minutes on the lowest shelf, until the topping is set and the bacon is crisp. Cut into 4 and serve with a salad.

   Tip: For best result and a crispier base, use the conventional oven setting.

Pork Saltimbocca

Serves 4   **5 mins preparation,
10 mins cooking using the hob**

Ingredients

4 x 100g pork escalopes
4 slices Parma ham
4 sage leaves
2 tablespoons plain flour
2 tablespoons olive oil
1 knob of butter
100ml Marsala wine

To serve

Sauted potatoes
Wilted spinach

Meaning 'jumps in the mouth' in Italian, saltimbocca is a quick, simple classic dish, usually made with veal. This version with pork is just as good, and the thin escalopes cook in virtually no time at all.

1. Place the pork escalopes on a chopping board, and wrap a slice of Parma ham around each one. Attach a sage leaf to the pork and ham with a cocktail stick.

2. Put the plain flour in a shallow dish, and coat the pork escalopes lightly on both sides, shaking off any excess.

3. In a large frying pan, heat the olive oil over a medium heat. Then fry the escalopes for 3 minutes on each side, until cooked through.

4. Just towards the end of the cooking, increase the temperature. Add the butter and Marsala, and sizzle them in the pan for just a minute to make a sauce. Serve with sauted potatoes and wilted spinach.

Duck Legs in Orange Sauce

Serves 4   **5 mins preparation,
20-25 mins cooking using the hob and oven**

Ingredients

3 oranges
4 duck legs
Sea salt and milled black pepper
80g granulated sugar
80ml white wine vinegar
2 tablespoons Grand Marnier
or Cointreau (optional)
2 teaspoons good quality
roast chicken gravy mix
300ml ready-made chicken stock

To serve

Fresh green garden vegetables

This classic orange sauce can be traced back to the 1800s, and was originally made with bitter 'bigarade' or Seville oranges. It is still officially called sauce bigarade, but is now made with sweet oranges and vinegar. Today, bigarade oranges are used mainly to make orange liqueurs.

1. Pre-heat the oven to 220°C/fan 200°C/gas mark 7. Line the oven tray with kitchen foil.

2. Remove the zest of one orange and juice all the oranges. Heat a large non-stick frying pan. Season the duck legs and place in the hot pan, skin side down. Cook over a high heat for 3 minutes, until golden. Flip over and cook for 2 more minutes.

3. Transfer the duck to the lined oven tray and bake for 20 to 25 minutes, depending on the size.

4. Meanwhile, discard the fat from the frying pan and sprinkle a thin layer of sugar into it. Place over a high heat and cook for 3-4 minutes, until the sugar turns to caramel.

5. Add the vinegar and orange juice – and the Grand Marnier or Cointreau, if you're using them. Be careful, as the liquid may bubble vigorously.

6. Boil down and reduce by half. Don't worry about any pieces of hard caramel; they will dissolve with the boiling.

7. Dissolve the gravy mix in 2 tablespoons of stock, and add this to the orange caramel sauce, along with the rest of the stock and the orange zest. Reduce the heat and simmer for 10 minutes, until thickened.

8. Remove the duck from the oven, transfer to a warm plate and cover with kitchen foil. Leave to rest for 5 minutes.

9. Serve the duck legs drizzled with the sauce and garnished with fresh green garden vegetables.

   Tip: Duck breasts are also delicious with this orange sauce. Pan-fry them for 5 minutes as above, and then roast for 10 minutes for medium rare.

Porcini and Fontina Risotto

Serves 4   **5 mins preparation, 25 mins cooking using the hob**

Ingredients

25g dried porcini mushrooms
1 knob of butter
2 tablespoons olive oil
250g mixed mushrooms, including chestnut, large flat and Portobello
3 shallots, finely chopped
1 garlic clove, finely chopped
A few sprigs fresh thyme, chopped
350g risotto rice
300ml white wine
1 litre hot vegetable stock
100g fontina cheese, diced
1 handful flat-leaf parsley, finely chopped

You can't beat a rich, creamy, cheesy risotto. Adding dried porcini mushrooms to this recipe really intensifies the flavour.

1. Place the dried porcini in a bowl, and pour boiling water over them. Leave to soak for about 10 minutes.

2. Meanwhile, heat the butter and 1 tablespoon of the olive oil in a saucepan, and fry the other mushrooms until golden. Remove from the pan, and keep to one side.

3. Add the remaining olive oil to the pan, and fry the shallots for a few minutes until they begin to soften. Add the garlic and thyme and cook for a minute longer.

4. Drain the porcini mushrooms and chop roughly. Add them to the pan with the shallots, and mix together well.

5. Stir in the rice, and add the wine. Let this bubble rapidly, until the rice has absorbed the wine – it will take about 2 minutes.

6. Gradually add the hot stock to the pan, a ladleful at a time, letting the rice absorb each ladleful before adding the next. Keep doing this until all the liquid is absorbed – this will be around 20 minutes.

7. Gently stir in the fried mushrooms, fontina and parsley, and cover the pan. Let the risotto sit for 3 minutes before ladling into serving bowls.

Potato, Chard and Pecorino Bake

Serves 4   10 mins preparation, 20 mins cooking using the hob and oven

Ingredients

350g chard
400g potatoes, peeled
and thinly sliced
1 knob of butter
2 garlic cloves, finely sliced
Sea salt and milled black pepper
300ml double cream
75g Pecorino cheese, grated

A potato and vegetable dish in one. This creamy bake is especially good with roast chicken.

1. Pre-heat the oven to 200ºC/fan 180ºC/gas mark 6.

2. Strip the chard leaves from the stalks, and keep to one side. Cut the stalks into sticks, about 6cm long.

3. Bring a pan of water to the boil, and cook the potatoes for 4 minutes. Then add the chard sticks, and cook for 1 minute more. Add the leaves, cook for another minute, just until they've wilted. Drain and keep to one side.

4. Heat the butter in a small, 1 litre ovenproof dish. Add the garlic and cook for a minute, until it turns a light golden colour.

5. Add the chard sticks, leaves and potatoes, tossing well with the garlic, season with salt and pepper.

6. Pour the double cream over, and scatter with grated Pecorino. Bake for 15 minutes, until bubbling and golden, and serve straight from the dish.

Pears in Red Wine and Redcurrant Syrup

Serves 4   **5 mins preparation, 25 mins cooking using the hob**

Ingredients

1 orange
1 lemon
1 bottle red wine
300g redcurrant jelly
1 large cinnamon stick
10 black peppercorns
4 ripe pears

To serve

Almond biscuits

This is the perfect dessert for a winter meal, and any leftover liquid is lovely in white wine or champagne.

1. Using a vegetable peeler, cut 2 long (10cm) strips of zest from the orange and 2 from the lemon. (Reserve the fruit for other recipes).

2. Place the wine, jelly, orange and lemon zest, cinnamon and peppercorns in the saucepan. Bring to a simmer and cook for a few minutes to dissolve the jelly.

3. Peel the pears with a vegetable peeler, keeping the stems intact. As you finish peeling each one, place it in the simmering wine mixture. Simmer the pears for 12-15 minutes. Check they're tender all the way through by piercing with a knife.

4. Ladle all the poaching liquid into a large frying pan (where it will evaporate faster) and boil for 10 minutes, until the volume is reduced by half and the texture becomes syrupy. Pour this back over the pears and leave to cool.

5. Serve the pears lukewarm or cold, drizzled with the syrup. Almond biscuits go nicely with them.

   Tip: The golden rule for cooking with wine is, "do not cook with a wine you would not drink". Make sure the red wine tastes good before you use it!

Thin Apple Tart

Serves 4   **10 mins preparation, 20 mins baking using the oven**

Ingredients

320g pack ready rolled
all butter puff pastry
2 large, Golden Delicious apples
2 tablespoons apricot jam
30g butter, melted
3 tablespoons icing sugar

To serve

Crème fraîche

With very finely cut apples, coated with butter and sugar several times during baking, this classic tart really melts in the mouth.

1. Pre-heat the oven to 220°C/fan 200°C/gas mark 7. Line a baking tray with baking parchment.

2. Unroll the pastry. Using a 23cm plate as a guide, cut out a circle of pastry and place it on the lined baking tray. Keep the leftover pastry.

3. Prick the pastry base all over with a fork; this will prevent it from shrinking.

4. Core and peel the apples. Cut them in half lengthways, then cut each half into very thin slices (about 3mm).

5. Spread the apricot jam over the circle of pastry. Arrange the apple slices over the top, overlapping them slightly, in 2 concentric rings to make the shape of a flower. Brush with melted butter and, using a tea strainer or fine sieve, dust generously with about 1 tablespoon of icing sugar.

6. Bake for 10 minutes, then remove from the oven, brush with butter again and dust with more icing sugar. Return to the oven for 5 more minutes, then repeat with the butter and sugar. Cook for a final 5 minutes until the tart is nicely caramelised on top. Serve lukewarm with a scoop of crème fraiche.

   Tip: For best results and a crispier base, use the conventional oven setting.

Rice Pudding with Warm Cherry Sauce

Serves 8

**10 mins preparation,
50 mins cooking using the hob**

Ingredients

1.5 litres semi-skimmed milk
1 vanilla pod, split
250g pudding rice
2 tablespoons brown sugar
200ml double cream
50g blanched almonds,
roughly chopped

For the cherry sauce

700g cherries, fresh or
tinned and drained
150g caster sugar
1 teaspoon sea salt
1 vanilla pod, split
Juice of 1 lemon
200ml water plus 2
tablespoons for paste
2 tablespoons cornflour

Traditionally, this dish is served in Scandinavia on Christmas Eve, when it helps provide the entertainment. A whole almond is hidden in the centre of the pudding, and whoever finds it gets a present. This isn't in this version, but feel free to put it in yours!

1. In a large pan, heat the milk and add the vanilla pod. Bring the milk to the boil, and just before it boils, add the rice. Turn the heat down and simmer for 25 minutes, stirring frequently.

2. Remove the pan from the heat, cover with a lid, and leave for 10 minutes.

3. Remove the lid and stir in the sugar. Leave the pudding to cool, then transfer it to a large bowl.

4. In a separate bowl, whip the cream until it forms soft peaks.

5. Gently fold half of the whipped cream into the rice. When the mixture is smooth, add the remaining cream, then fold in the almonds. Spoon the mixture into a serving bowl, cover and chill in the fridge.

6. To make the sauce, put the cherries, sugar, salt, vanilla pod, lemon juice and water in a pan. Bring to the boil and simmer over a low heat for 15 minutes.

7. Mix the cornflour and 2 tablespoons of water together to make a thin paste, and slowly add this to the cherry sauce, stirring continuously until it thickens and the sauce comes to the boil.

8. Spoon the cold rice pudding into bowls, and serve with the warm cherry sauce.

Hot Buttered Rum

Serves 4   **5 mins preparation,
2-3 mins cooking using the hob**

Ingredients

4 teaspoons unsalted
butter, softened
4 teaspoons maple syrup
2 teaspoons ground allspice
200ml golden rum
Apple juice to top up the glasses
4 cinnamon sticks
Nutmeg, freshly grated

This American classic is popular throughout autumn and winter. It has a long history and several variations, but this recipe is delicious with the comforting flavours of maple syrup, apple juice and cinnamon.

1. Divide the butter between 4 heatproof glasses. Add the maple syrup, allspice and rum.

2. Warm the apple juice in a pan, and use it to top up the glasses. Stir with a spoon until all the ingredients are combined.

3. Warm the cinnamon sticks in a frying pan and place one in each of the glasses.

4. Sprinkle the rum with grated nutmeg and serve immediately.

Tis' the season!

The festive season is always a wonderful time to bring friends and family together and gives you the perfect excuse to cook all sorts of comforting recipes. We love anything slow cooked, roasted or baked for maximum cosiness. From Baked Mushrooms with Garlic Butter to a Roast Goose with all the trimmings and who could resist a Chocolate and Raspberry Yule Log? What could be better on a cold winter's night, than snuggling next to a warm fire, nestling a mug of Hot Chocolate and a plate full of Mincemeat Crumble Pies?

flavour
AT ITS BEST

Brussel Sprouts, Butternut
Squash, Cabbages, Celery,
Onions, Potatoes, Sweet
Potatoes, Winter Squash.

Baked Mushrooms with Garlic Butter

Serves 2 **10 mins preparation,**
15 mins cooking using the oven

Ingredients

12 medium chestnut mushrooms
100g butter at room temperature
20g shallots, roughly chopped
2 large garlic cloves, crushed
20g parsley, roughly chopped
¼ teaspoon nutmeg, freshly grated
¼ teaspoon sea salt
15g ground almonds
Milled black pepper

To serve

Crusty baguette

If you love mushrooms, this is the perfect way to eat them. Make sure you have plenty of crusty bread to mop up the buttery juices.

1. Pre-heat the oven to 200°C/fan 180°C/gas mark 6. Place a baking tray on the lowest shelf.

2. Clean the mushrooms – but don't use running water, as mushrooms absorb it like sponges. Instead, wipe any dirt away with slightly damp kitchen paper.

3. Trim off the stems, right down to the base.

4. Place the butter, shallots, garlic, parsley, nutmeg, salt, almonds and 10 grinds of the peppermill in a food processor. Process until well blended. Alternatively, chop the shallots, garlic and parsley very finely and incorporate into the butter along with the nutmeg, salt and almonds.

5. Fill each mushroom cap with a heaped tablespoon of the garlic butter and place in the muffin tin. Put the tin on the hot baking tray and cook for 15 minutes until the butter bubbles.

6. Spoon the mushrooms and butter juices onto 2 plates, and serve with a crusty baguette.

   Tip: Use a muffin tin rather than a flat tray so the melting butter bastes the mushrooms instead of spreading out.

Fisherman's Soup

Serves 4   20 mins preparation, 45-50 mins cooking using the hob

Ingredients

60ml olive oil
2 onions, peeled and finely chopped
2 green peppers, finely chopped
2 garlic cloves, peeled and grated
400g tinned chopped tomatoes
2 tablespoons sweet paprika
800ml fish stock
Sea salt and milled black pepper
800g fish fillets (carp, brown trout, perch or pike), cut into 3cm pieces
200g soured cream
4 tablespoons fresh flat-leaf parsley, roughly chopped

To serve

Crusty white bread

Traditionally, this dish is made with freshwater fish, such as pike, carp or perch. These fish can be an acquired taste, so you can replace them with brown trout or even a white fish like cod or haddock.

1. Heat the oil in a large saucepan over a medium heat. Add the onion, green pepper and garlic, and cook for 2-3 minutes, until softened and the onions turn translucent.

2. Add the tomatoes and cook for a further 5 minutes.

3. Add the paprika and stir for 1 minute.

4. Add the fish stock and simmer for 30 minutes. Season with salt and pepper.

5. Add the fish pieces and simmer for a further 5 minutes, until the fish is cooked through. Don't stir the soup too much, or you'll break the fish chunks.

6. Season again and divide between 4 serving bowls. Top with soured cream and parsley, and serve with crusty white bread.

Goat's Cheese and Thyme Scented Fig Toasts

Makes 24   **30 mins preparation, 8-10 mins cooking using the hob**

Ingredients

6 fresh or dried figs, quartered
6 tablespoons soft brown sugar
200ml red wine
½ teaspoon fresh thyme leaves, plus 1 tablespoon for garnish
Sea salt
1 baguette, cut diagonally into 24 slices
3 tablespoons olive oil
250g fresh goat's cheese
Milled black pepper

These little toasts will brighten up a chilly winter's day. They feature a delicious fig compote, which you can also make as a quick chutney for your Christmas table. It's wonderful with ham or Stilton too and will keep in the fridge for 5 days in a sealed container.

1. In a small saucepan, combine the figs, sugar, wine and thyme. Add a pinch of salt.

2. Bring the pan to the boil, then reduce to a simmer for 8-10 minutes, until the mixture has thickened into a compote. Put to one side to cool.

3. Meanwhile, brush each baguette slice with oil and toast each side.

4. Spread each slice with goat's cheese and top with a spoonful of the compote. Garnish with a little more thyme, season with pepper and serve immediately.

Porchetta

Serves 6-8   30 mins preparation, 3.5-4 hours cooking using the oven

Ingredients

2.5-3kg pork belly with ribs removed
15g sea salt
2 tablespoons milled black pepper
15g fresh rosemary, chopped
15g fresh sage, chopped
2 tablespoons fennel seeds
Zest of 1 lemon
Zest of 1 orange
4 garlic cloves, peeled and grated
1 tablespoon olive oil
2-3 tablespoons runny honey

To serve

Roasted rosemary potatoes
Green vegetables

Porchetta is rolled roast pork stuffed with fennel and herbs and is an Italian classic. Serve hot or cold, it's perfect as part of a Boxing Day buffet. Great with roasted rosemary, potatoes and green vegetables.

1. Pre-heat the oven to 220°C/fan 200°C/gas mark 7.

2. Lay the pork belly on a work surface, skin side down. Sprinkle with half the salt and pepper, and all the rosemary, sage, fennel seeds, lemon and orange zest, and garlic. Rub the mixture into the meat, and leave for 15 minutes so the flavours can infuse.

3. With the longest side of the meat towards you, roll it up. You should end up with the seam at the bottom. Get one piece of string and tie the meat around the middle. Then tie the rest of the joint with the remaining pieces of string, leaving even gaps between each one.

4. Rub the top of the meat with the oil and the remaining salt and pepper. Place in a large roasting tin, and put in the oven for 20 minutes.

5. Turn the oven down to 150°C/fan 130°C/gas mark 2. Cover the meat with foil, and roast for 3½ hours. (If you want crispy crackling, leave the foil off, but the meat will be drier).

6. Take the porchetta out of the oven. Mix the honey with some of the juices from the pan, and pour this over the meat. Leave for 5 minutes.

7. Serve with roasted rosemary potatoes and green vegetables, such as kale.

Roast Goose

Serves 6   45 mins preparation, 3 hours 45 mins cooking using the oven and hob

Ingredients

325g Hungarian sausage,
casings removed (or any favourite
pork sausage)
60ml butter
1 onion, peeled and
roughly chopped
2 celery sticks, sliced
200g bread, torn into small chunks
2 large apples, cored and
roughly chopped
½ teaspoon dried marjoram
Sea salt and milled black pepper
2.5-3.5kg fresh whole goose
Juice of ½ lemon
4 sprigs fresh thyme
1 sprig fresh bay leaves
2 sprigs of fresh rosemary
1 onion, peeled and cut
into quarters
6 apples for garnish
50g butter, melted
35g demerara sugar

Goose is the traditional centrepiece for Christmas dinner. It's rich, tasty meat makes a nice change from turkey – and in this recipe, the spicy stuffing and caramelised apples add a range of festive flavours.

1. Pre-heat the oven to 180°C/fan 160°C/gas mark 4.

2. In a large frying pan, fry the sausage meat over a medium heat for 2-3 minutes, until browned. Remove from the pan, drain on kitchen paper and put in a bowl.

3. Add the butter to the frying pan, return to the heat and add the onion and celery. Cook for 5 minutes, until the onion is soft and translucent.

4. Add the onion and celery to the sausage meat, and stir in the bread chunks, apple and marjoram. Season with salt and pepper. Roll the mixture into walnut size balls, place on a roasting tray and chill in the fridge.

5. Rub the goose with the lemon juice and season with salt and pepper. Fill the cavity with thyme, bay, rosemary and the onion quarters.

6. Put the goose on a large cooking rack on top of a large roasting tray.

7. Cover the goose with foil and roast for 1½ hours. Take it out of the oven and carefully ladle all the fat out of the tin. Put the foil back and roast the goose for a further 1½ hours.
   Then baste the bird with some of the rendered fat and cook for 30 minutes without the foil.

8. 15 minutes before the goose is ready, halve the apples and brush with melted butter and sprinkle with demerara sugar. Place on the baking tray with the stuffing balls and cook in the oven for 30 minutes.

9. When the goose is ready, let it rest for 15 minutes, then serve with the roast apple and stuffing balls.

Artichoke Tart

Serves 6   20 mins preparation,
50 mins - 1 hour cooking using the hob and oven

Ingredients

4 tablespoons olive oil
1 onion, peeled and finely chopped
2 garlic cloves, peeled and grated
400g tinned artichoke hearts
3 eggs
100g green olives, roughly chopped
100g Parmesan cheese, grated
2 tablespoons milk
2 tablespoons fresh parsley,
roughly chopped
1 tablespoon fresh basil,
roughly torn
Milled black pepper
30g breadcrumbs

To serve

Green salad

The combination of olives, garlic and onion, make this an incredibly tasty recipe for lunch or supper.

1. Pre-heat the oven to 190ºC/fan 170ºC/gas mark 5.

2. In a large frying pan, heat 2 tablespoons of oil and add the onion. Cook for 10 minutes over a low heat, until the onions are soft and translucent.

3. Add the garlic and continue cooking for 5 minutes, until the onions are golden.

4. Drain the artichokes and dry on kitchen paper. Cut each one into quarters.

5. In a large bowl, beat the eggs and add the cooked onion and garlic, the artichoke quarters, olives, 75g of Parmesan and the milk. Add the parsley and basil, and season with pepper.

6. Grease an ovenproof baking dish with 1 tablespoon of oil, and pour the mixture into it. Sprinkle with breadcrumbs, the left over Parmesan and drizzle with the remaining oil.

7. Cook in the oven for 35-40 minutes, until the top is golden.

8. Serve hot or cold, with a green salad.

Bream with Salsa Verde

Serves 4   15 mins preparation, 20 mins cooking using the hob

Ingredients

400g baby new potatoes
50g plain flour
2 teaspoons smoked paprika
Sea salt and milled black pepper
4 sea bream fillets
4 tablespoons olive oil
100g chorizo, cut into small pieces
400g baby spinach
Juice of 1 lemon

For the salsa verde

1 bunch fresh flat-leaf parsley
1 bunch fresh mint
2 garlic cloves, peeled and crushed
1½ tablespoons capers, rinsed
1 medium green chilli, deseeded and chopped
Juice of ½ lemon
200ml extra virgin olive oil
Sea salt

Christmas is a time for treating yourself to foods you probably wouldn't eat every day. So this sea bream recipe is perfect for the festive season.

1. First make the salsa verde, by putting the parsley, mint, garlic, capers, chilli and lemon juice in a food processor until well blended. Then slowly pour in the oil, until well combined. Season, place in a bowl, cover and keep in the fridge.

2. Boil the potatoes until just tender. Drain, and keep them warm.

3. Mix together the flour, paprika, salt and pepper. Dust the bream with the flour mixture, and shake off any excess.

4. Add 2 tablespoons of oil to a large frying pan, and cook the fish, skin side down, over a medium heat for 3-5 minutes. Turn the fish over and cook for a further minute.

5. Meanwhile, heat another large frying pan and add the remaining oil. Add the chorizo and cook for 2-3 minutes.

6. Add the potatoes and cook for 2 minutes.

7. Add the spinach and cook for a further minute until the spinach wilts. Squeeze the lemon juice over the spinach and check the seasoning.

8. Serve the fish with the potato and chorizo mixture, and a spoonful of the salsa verde.

Chocolate and Raspberry Yule Log

Serves 10   **25 mins preparation, 12-14 mins cooking using the hob and oven**

Ingredients
150g caster sugar
6 large eggs, separated
250g chocolate (70% cocoa)
Icing sugar for dusting

For the cream filling
300ml double cream,
lightly whipped
200g raspberries

For the chocolate butter cream
150g unsalted butter, softened
225g icing sugar
25g cocoa powder, sifted
2 tablespoons semi-skimmed milk

In France, the yule log dessert is an even bigger part of Christmas than it is here. The French version features a cream and raspberry filling, which contrasts nicely with the rich, flourless chocolate cake and butter cream.

1. Pre-heat the oven to 180°C/fan 160°C/gas mark 4.
2. Line a 23cm x 33cm Swiss roll tin with greaseproof paper or baking parchment.
3. In a large bowl, whisk together the caster sugar and egg yolks, until you have a thick, creamy mixture.
4. In another bowl, melt the chocolate over a pan of simmering water. Remove the chocolate from the heat, let it cool for 5 minutes, then stir it into the sugar and egg mixture.
5. In a separate, large bowl, whisk the egg whites until they become stiff.
6. With a large metal spoon, stir a spoonful of the egg whites into the chocolate mixture, then gently fold in the remaining egg whites.
7. Pour this batter into the prepared tin, and bake for 12-14 minutes, until the cake has risen and is firm to the touch. Leave to cool.
8. Meanwhile, make the butter cream by beating the butter, icing sugar and cocoa together. Add the milk, and continue to beat until smooth and fluffy. Cover with cling film and keep to one side.
9. Lay a sheet of baking parchment on a board. Turn the cake onto this, and gently peel away the lining paper.
10. Spread the whipped double cream over the cake, then scatter with raspberries. Starting with the long side facing you, roll the cake, using the baking parchment to help you. Transfer the cake to a serving dish.
11. Cut off a third of the cake, then cut one end of the shorter piece at an angle, so you can fit it onto the side of the main log, towards one end, to form a branch. Use a little of the butter cream for 'glue' to stick your branch on.
12. Coat the log with the rest of the butter cream, and use a fork to create a log effect. Dust with icing sugar and serve.

Cranberry Topped Cheesecake

Serves 8   25 mins preparation, 1 hour cooking using the oven and hob

A classic layer cheesecake recipe gets the festive treatment with this luscious cranberry and Cointreau topping.

Ingredients

50g unsalted butter, plus a little extra for greasing
150g digestive or ginger snap biscuits
600g full-fat cream cheese
3 large eggs
300ml soured cream
175g caster sugar
1 tablespoon cornflour
1 teaspoon vanilla bean paste
Juice and grated zest of 1 unwaxed lemon
100g Greek-style yoghurt

For the topping

350g cranberries
175g caster sugar
1 teaspoon vanilla bean paste
2 tablespoons Cointreau or Grand Marnier
Juice of ½ orange
1-2 teaspoons cornflour

1. Pre-heat the oven to 170°C/150°C fan/gas mark 3. Butter the base of the tin and line with a disc of buttered baking parchment.

2. Crush the biscuits in a food processor or put them in a freezer bag and bash with a rolling pin. Place in a bowl.

3. Melt the butter and mix into the biscuit crumbs. Place in the prepared tin and press into an even layer over the base. Bake on the middle shelf of the oven for 5 minutes.

4. In a bowl, combine the cream cheese, eggs, half of the soured cream, 125g of caster sugar and the tablespoon of cornflour. Blitz until smooth, then add the vanilla, lemon juice and zest and blitz again.

5. Carefully pour the mixture into the tin. Place on a baking sheet and bake on the middle shelf of the oven for 35 minutes, or until just set.

6. Remove from the oven and leave to rest for 10 minutes – but keep the oven on.

7. Meanwhile, beat together the remaining soured cream and 50g of caster sugar with the Greek-style yoghurt. Carefully spoon this mixture on top of the cheesecake and return to the oven for a further 15 minutes, or until set but not coloured.

8. Remove the cheesecake from the oven and leave to cool completely before chilling in the fridge.

9. To prepare the topping, place half of the cranberries in a pan with the sugar, vanilla and Cointreau or Grand Marnier. Cook over a medium heat, until the cranberries burst and start to release their juice. Add the remaining cranberries and cook for a moment longer to soften them. Mix the orange juice and cornflour together in a small bowl. Add to the cranberry mixture, stirring constantly as it slightly thickens.

10. Remove from the heat, pour into a bowl and leave until cold.

11. Carefully remove the cheesecake from the tin and place on a serving plate. Top with the cranberry compote.

Mincemeat Crumble Pies

Makes 24 — 30 mins preparation plus 1 hour chilling, 20-25 mins cooking using the oven

Ingredients

For the pastry

150g plain flour,
plus extra for rolling out
½ teaspoon baking powder
25g caster sugar
1 pinch salt
75g unsalted butter,
chilled and diced
75g cream cheese
50g ground almonds
1 medium egg yolk
1 tablespoon milk

For the crumble topping

75g light soft brown sugar
75g plain flour
1 teaspoon ground cinnamon
50g finely chopped almonds
40g unsalted butter, melted
400g luxury mincemeat
Icing sugar for dusting

The cream cheese pastry in this recipe takes mince pies to another level – especially when paired with a tasty nutty crumble topping.

1. To make the pastry, place the flour, baking powder, sugar and salt in the food processor bowl. Add the butter, and use the pulse button to rub it into the dry ingredients, until the mixture resembles fine sand.

2. Add the cream cheese, ground almonds, egg yolk and milk, and mix again until a dough starts to form. Place in a mixing bowl and use your hands to make a neat ball – but do not overwork it. Flatten into a disc, cover with cling film and leave in the fridge for 1 hour.

3. Lightly dust the work surface with plain flour. Divide the dough in two and roll out one half until it is around 2mm thick. Using the pastry cutter, stamp out as many discs from the dough as you can. Use them to line the bun trays, pressing gently with your fingers.

4. Gather the dough scraps together and set aside. Roll out the second half of the dough and stamp out more pastry discs, continuing to line the bun trays. Gather all the dough scraps together and press gently into a ball. Roll this out and stamp out more discs – you should aim for 24 pastry cases in total.

5. Chill the pastry in the fridge for 30 minutes while you pre-heat the oven to 180°C/160°C fan/gas mark 4 and make the crumble topping. To do this, place the sugar, flour, cinnamon and almonds in a bowl, then add the melted butter and use your fingers to combine.

6. Spoon the mincemeat into each pastry case and top with a little of the crumble mixture. Bake on the middle shelf of the oven for about 20 minutes or until golden brown. Leave to cool in the bun trays for 10 minutes, then remove carefully and transfer to a wire rack to cool completely. Serve the pies warm and dust with a little icing sugar.

Christmas Punch

Serves 12   **35 mins preparation, 10 mins cooking using the hob**

Ingredients

225g caster sugar
900ml strongly brewed
black tea, hot
Juice of 4 lemons
Juice of 3 oranges
8 cloves
1 cinnamon stick
2 bottles red wine
225ml rum

To serve

Lemon and orange slices

If you've ever visited a German Christmas market, you're probably familiar with this punch consisting of tea, red wine, rum, lemons and oranges. Try making it at home and enjoy the wonderful festive aromas it creates.

1. In a large pan, mix together the sugar and tea. Add the lemon juice, orange juice, cloves and cinnamon stick. Stir until the sugar dissolves completely.

2. Add the red wine. Heat the mixture until it just comes to the boil, then turn the heat off.
   Let it sit to infuse for 30 minutes.

3. When you're ready to serve, gently heat the rum in a separate pan, being careful not to let it boil. When hot, add to the tea and wine mixture.

4. Remove the cloves and cinnamon stick. Pour the punch into mugs, and serve it hot with fresh lemon and orange slices.

Cinnamon Custard

Ingredients

600ml whole milk
½ vanilla pod or 1 teaspoon vanilla bean paste
1 large cinnamon stick
5 medium egg yolks
50g golden caster sugar
2 tablespoons brandy (optional)

1. Pour the milk into a saucepan. Split the vanilla pod in half and add to the pan along with the cinnamon stick. Bring slowly to the boil then remove from the heat and leave to one side for about 30 minutes so the milk becomes infused with the vanilla and cinnamon.

2. In a large bowl, beat the egg yolks and sugar until pale and creamy. Reheat the milk and pour onto the egg mixture, whisking constantly until smooth. Pour the custard back into the pan, place over a low heat and stir constantly until the custard is thick enough to coat the back of a spoon and add the brandy if using – do not let it boil or you might scramble the eggs.

3. Strain into a jug and serve immediately.

Clementine and Brandy Butter

Ingredients

175g unsalted butter, at room temperature
75g icing sugar, sifted
50g soft light brown sugar
¼ teaspoon ground cinnamon
1 good grating of nutmeg
Finely grated zest of 1 clementine
3 tablespoons brandy

1. Beat the soft butter with both sugars until light, creamy and smooth. Add the cinnamon, nutmeg and clementine zest and mix again.

2. Gradually add the brandy, mixing well until thoroughly incorporated. Serve at room temperature.

Hot Chocolate

Ingredients

150g dark chocolate (68%)
50g milk chocolate
350ml semi-skimmed milk
100ml double cream
1 cinnamon stick
2-3 tablespoons maple syrup or clear honey
1 teaspoon vanilla extract
1 pinch salt
Whipped cream and marshmallows to serve

1. Chop both of the chocolates and place in a mixing bowl or jug.

2. In a medium-sized saucepan, combine the milk and cream. Add the cinnamon stick, maple syrup or honey, vanilla extract and salt. Slowly bring to the boil over a low heat to let the cinnamon infuse the milk and cream.

3. Pour the hot milk mixture over the chopped chocolate and whisk until smooth. Return the mixture to the pan and gently reheat, whisking constantly, until just below boiling point. Pour into mugs or heatproof glasses, (depending on the size of these, this recipe is enough for at least two servings). Top with whipped cream and marshmallows and serve immediately.

About Howdens Joinery

Our story began in 1995 with a commitment to provide leading kitchen designs at the best local price to trade professionals and their customers. Today, we are the UK's largest designer and manufacturer of fitted kitchens, transforming more than 400,000 homes every year.

LOCAL EXPERTISE

An experienced builder has a unique understanding of their local area and the homes within it. We respect trade professionals' know-how and workmanship, trusting them to install our kitchens to the highest possible standards. In turn, they trust us to have exactly the stock that they need at each of our 670 local depots.

DESIGN AND INNOVATION

We stay at the forefront of kitchen design, technology and innovation so you can be certain that your new kitchen will meet the demands of modern life. Traditional craftsmanship and rigorous testing ensure that our kitchens are designed and manufactured above and beyond industry standards. And key trends from around the world are incorporated into our styles, so we can make sure that if you want a certain look or feel, together with your builder, we can make it a reality.

QUALITY & SERVICE

From the day your builder installs your kitchen, your cabinets are guaranteed for 25 years, and all of our cabinet doors are guaranteed for five years to give you total peace of mind. All of our appliances come with a minimum of a year manufacturer's guarantee. If you choose one of our Lamona appliances we will guarantee it for two years and for five years on Lamona oven door glass.

HOWDENS JOINERY CO.

MAKING SPACE MORE VALUABLE

LAMONA

Exclusive to Howdens Joinery Co.

Contemporary

Shaker

Your Complete Kitchen

Everyone has their own vision of their dream kitchen. Whether it is contemporary greys, traditional rustic trends or a timeless classic, you can find your favourite look within one of our three kitchen collections: Contemporary, Shaker and Universal.

Now you have chosen your favourite kitchen style, you need to consider the features that will add function, flair and versatility to your kitchen.
Select from our extensive range of appliances, worktops, storage solutions, sinks, taps, flooring and handles. Add a personal signature to your new kitchen with lighting, splashbacks, backboards, waste solutions and even plinth heaters.

We have everything you need to bring your kitchen to life.

**DOWNLOAD OR ORDER
YOUR KITCHEN BROCHURE
AT HOWDENS.COM**

Universal